MONUMENTAL MILESTONES
GREAT EVENTS OF MODERN TIMES

Building the Panama Canal

Construction of the Panama Canal took about thirty-four years, starting with the French in 1881 and finally completed by the United States in 1914.

Mitchell Lane
PUBLISHERS

P.O. Box 196
Hockessin, Delaware 19707

Titles in the Series

MONUMENTAL MILESTONES
GREAT EVENTS OF MODERN TIMES

Building the Panama Canal

In 2007, expansion of the canal locks began. Completion was estimated for 2015.

Russell Roberts

Mitchell Lane
PUBLISHERS

Copyright © 2009 by Mitchell Lane Publishers, Inc. All rights reserved. No part of this book may be reproduced without written permission from the publisher. Printed and bound in the United States of America.

Printing   1   2   3   4   5   6   7   8   9

Library of Congress Cataloging-in-Publication Data
Roberts, Russell, 1953–
  Building the Panama Canal / by Russell Roberts.
    p. cm. — (Monumental milestones)
  Includes bibliographical references and index.
  ISBN 978-1-58415-692-5 (library bound)
  1. Panama Canal (Panama)—Design and construction—History—Juvenile literature.
I. Title.
  TC774.R63 2009
  386'.44—dc22

                                                  2008020928

ABOUT THE AUTHOR: Russell Roberts has written and published nearly 40 books for adults and children on a variety of subjects, including baseball, memory power, business, New Jersey history, and travel. He has written numerous books for Mitchell Lane Publishers, including *Nathaniel Hawthorne, Holidays and Celebrations in Colonial America, What's So Great About Daniel Boone, Poseidon, The Life and Times of Nostradamus,* and *The Lost Continent of Atlantis.* He lives in Bordentown, New Jersey, with his family and a fat, fuzzy, and crafty calico cat named Rusti.

PUBLISHER'S NOTE: This story is based on the author's extensive research, which he believes to be accurate. Documentation of such research is contained on page 46.

    The internet sites referenced herein were active as of the publication date. Due to the fleeting nature of some web sites, we cannot guarantee they will all be active when you are reading this book.

PLB

MONUMENTAL MILESTONES
GREAT EVENTS OF MODERN TIMES

Contents

Building the Panama Canal

Russell Roberts

*For Your Information

Count Ferdinand de Lesseps and part of his family in 1881. The tranquility of this family would soon be shattered by the Panama Canal.

In 1881 Ferdinand de Lesseps was a French hero, lionized for building the Suez Canal when no one believed it could be done. He tried to duplicate that success in Panama, with disastrous results.

Never to Smile Again

On December 15, 1888, a French newspaper editor walked along a sidewalk in Paris. He was searching for a house. He wanted to be the first person to tell the home's occupants something . . . something important . . . something earth-shattering.

As he walked, the editor passed horse-drawn carriages, ladies with parasols, and men in top hats. Finally he found the house he had been looking for—11 Avenue Montaigne. He went to the front door and knocked. Seconds later an old man appeared at the door. The man was in his eighties, but still seemed energetic and vigorous. He had white hair and a bushy white mustache with tips that extended off his face.

The man's name was Ferdinand de Lesseps, but he was often called by another title: Le Grand Français (the Great Frenchman). He was a hero in France—the man who had headed the building of the miraculous Suez Canal in Egypt. The canal had been a feat that many thought was impossible, but de Lesseps had done it, and Frenchmen everywhere basked in the glory.

Now he was deeply involved in another canal project: the digging of a canal across the Isthmus of Panama, a strip of land owned by the South American nation of Colombia. The work had been plagued by hardships: Landslides, disease, rainy weather, and many other problems had turned the project into a nightmare. After seven years, the canal still was not finished.

The work had been costly. Millions of francs had already been spent. Many millions more were needed to continue. The Panama Canal Company that de Lesseps had founded to dig the canal was bankrupt. It needed more money to continue operating or it would cease to exist.

Even steeper than the financial cost was the human price. Some 20,000 men had died since the digging began on February 1, 1881. Some had been

When the first ships sailed through the Suez Canal in 1869, it marked the triumphant conclusion of one of the world's great engineering feats.

The Suez Canal had long been a dream, from ancient times through Napoleon. It took de Lesseps nearly 11 years, but he turned this dream into a reality in 1869. The canal's opening led to increased and more efficient trade worldwide.

killed in construction accidents. Others had been killed by jungle animals like snakes. Many had been killed by diseases such as malaria and yellow fever.

After all the money that had been spent and all the people who had died, only eleven miles of canal out of fifty had been dug. Now de Lesseps wanted—needed—more money to continue. He was certain that patriotic pride would not allow France or its people to abandon the project.

He was wrong. Everyone in France knew that the project was going badly, and few wanted to invest more funds into it. In addition, France was in the midst of an economic depression. Money was tight.

In a last-ditch attempt to raise funds, de Lesseps had gotten government permission to hold a public lottery. The lottery would sell bonds to the public. The idea was that when the canal was complete and generating revenue, the bonds would be worth far more than people had paid for them. That was how it had worked for the Suez Canal stockholders. Many had become wealthy.

The Panama Canal bonds had not sold well. It did not help that on the day the bonds went on sale, someone started a rumor that de Lesseps had died, scaring the public.[1]

Le Grand Français had refused to admit defeat. In the autumn of 1888 he had gone on a strenuous tour of personal appearances throughout France, urging people to buy the bonds. It was an incredible feat of strength and willpower for the eighty-three-year-old. It demonstrated how badly he wanted to finish the canal.

On December 2, de Lesseps had personally challenged his countrymen: "I appeal to all Frenchmen. Your fates are in your own hands. Decide!"[2]

The public did decide, but not the way de Lesseps had hoped. At least 400,000 bonds needed to be sold to raise sufficient funds. Fewer than 200,000 were purchased.

The Great Frenchman had one more card left to play. He asked the French government to pass a bill that would let his canal company stop paying

The canal's success had made some bond-holders rich. But in Panama the project's troubles made people reluctant to buy the bonds. Ultimately de Lesseps ran out of money.

An 1881 French Panama Canal bond sold by Ferdinand de Lesseps.

A statue of Ferdinand de Lesseps was erected at the Mediterranean entrance to the Suez Canal in 1899.

Ferdinand de Lesseps was not an engineer. Nevertheless, he built the Suez Canal, which was an engineering marvel. Later, his lack of engineering expertise doomed the Panama Canal project.

its debts and making interest payments for three months. De Lesseps hoped that the reprieve would enable him to form a new company and resume the digging.

On December 15, 1888, the French government rejected the bill. This was the news the editor was bringing to de Lesseps. He was there to tell him that his dream of building the Panama Canal was dead.

When the newspaperman told the old man about the vote, all the color drained from de Lesseps's face. He turned pale as a ghost. He knew what the news meant, but he could not believe it. He could not believe that his country would abandon the canal project.

"It is impossible! It is shameful!"[3] he whispered.

It was true. De Lesseps's dream for the Panama Canal was dead. According to legend, from that day until the end of his life six years later, Ferdinand de Lesseps never smiled again.[4]

The idea of building a canal through Panama to link the Pacific and Atlantic oceans was hundreds of years old before the first shovel broke ground.

In 1513, Spanish explorer Vasco Núñez de Balboa landed on the Atlantic coast side of Panama. A group of friendly natives told him of a fabulous body of water on the other side of the isthmus. For over a month Balboa and his crew chopped their way through the jungle, battling disease, dodging the poison arrows of unfriendly natives, and suffering from the stifling heat. In late September the Spaniards began climbing a hill. Balboa ordered his men to wait while he continued alone to the top. At the summit he became the first European to see the Pacific Ocean from its eastern shore, shimmering like a piece of glass in the distance.

In the report he sent to Spain, Balboa noted the narrowness of the Isthmus of Panama—it was about fifty miles across. He recommended that a trail be built between the two oceans. He also mentioned the idea one of his engineers had for building a connecting waterway.

Bronze statue of Vasco Núñez de Balboa in Madrid, Spain, made by sculptor Enrique Pérez Comendador

Such a waterway would come in handy. After conquering the Aztecs in Mexico and the Incas in Peru, the Spaniards had loads of pillaged gold and silver. To get these riches home, the conquistadores had to go by ship all the way around the tip of South America, or by land to Spanish ports in the Caribbean Sea. Both ways were slow and dangerous.

In the 1530s, Spain's King Charles V considered the canal idea, but he didn't take action. His successor, Philip II, also thought about building a canal through the isthmus, but then decided that if God had wanted a canal there, there would already be one. Philip decreed that anybody who tried to build a canal would be put to death.

Finally, in the early 1800s, a German baron named Alexander von Humboldt revived interest in the canal by proposing nine possible routes. By this time Spain was no longer a world power. It stood by as stronger nations carried forward the idea of the Panama Canal.

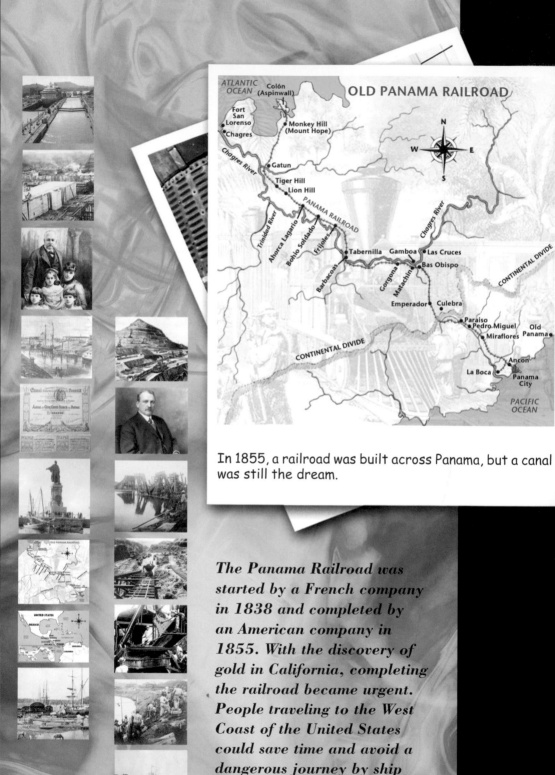

OLD PANAMA RAILROAD

ATLANTIC OCEAN

Colón (Aspinwall)

Fort San Lorenso
Chagres
Monkey Hill (Mount Hope)

Chagres River

Gatun

Tiger Hill
Lion Hill

PANAMA RAILROAD

Trinidad River
Ahorca Lagarto
Bohio Soldado
Frijoles
Barbacoa
Tabernilla
Gamboa
Las Cruces
Chagres River

Gorgona
Matachin
Bas Obispo

CONTINENTAL DIVIDE

Emperador
Culebra

CONTINENTAL DIVIDE

Paraiso
Pedro Miguel
Miraflores
Old Panama

Ancon

La Boca
Panama City

PACIFIC OCEAN

In 1855, a railroad was built across Panama, but a canal was still the dream.

The Panama Railroad was started by a French company in 1838 and completed by an American company in 1855. With the discovery of gold in California, completing the railroad became urgent. People traveling to the West Coast of the United States could save time and avoid a dangerous journey by ship around South America.

The French Attempt a Canal

Panama lies nine degrees above the equator. It is the southernmost nation in Central America and connects to the South American nation of Colombia. Shaped like an *s*, it is about 500 miles long and varies from 30 to 130 miles across.

Panama receives 105 inches of rainfall per year and has an average temperature of 80 degrees. These conditions promote the growth of dense, almost suffocating rain forests. One French surveyor described Panama as "a wilderness of jungle so thick that it is impossible to see ten feet in any direction, and so gloomy and stifling that it is difficult to breathe."[1]

When the rainfall is heavy, the jungle's streams and rivers rage. After two days of heavy rain in 1903, the Chagres River on the Atlantic side of the isthmus was a torrent sixty feet above sea level.[2] During the rainy season, its flow has been known to multiply 140 times.[3] The hot, humid environment is perfect for mosquitoes that carry yellow fever, malaria, and a host of other diseases.

Despite the obstacles, the short width of the isthmus beckoned. In 1838 France began building a railroad across Panama, which was still part of Colombia. The project was dogged by delay and had little sense of urgency.

Then in 1848, gold was discovered in California. Thousands of Americans left their homes and headed west to seek their fortunes. The journey was difficult. People could trek cross-country through undeveloped regions bristling with hostile natives, wild animals, and weather hazards such as sandstorms. Their other choice was to take a ship around the tip of South America and then up to California—a hazardous 13,000-mile journey that took five months.

Traveling across Panama would make it much faster to reach California. When the French railroad project floundered, an American company jumped

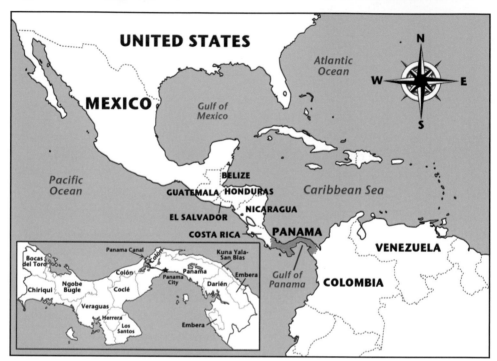

Panama seemed to be the natural choice for digging a canal. Yet it was not at all certain that the canal would be built in Panama. Several other locations—such as Nicaragua—were also considered.

in. The Panama Railroad Company completed a railway across Panama in 1855.

During construction of the railroad, interest in a canal intensified. Both Great Britain and the U.S. considered building a canal in the country of Nicaragua, to the north of Panama. England did not want the United States to establish a presence in Nicaragua. On January 1, 1849, a British gunboat appeared off the Nicaraguan coast.

The dispute was settled by diplomacy. In 1850 the two nations negotiated the Clayton-Bulwer Treaty. It specified that any canal built in Central America would be a shared project. The treaty became official American policy, but it did not completely stop U.S. leaders from continuing to pursue a canal. One of those leaders was President Ulysses S. Grant.

In July 1852, while Grant was still a captain in the army, he led the Fourth Infantry across Panama to reach their next post in California. The detail numbered approximately 700 troops and their families. They arrived in Aspinwall (later called Colón) on the Atlantic side of Panama. Grant immediately hated it, thanks to the blazing sun and drenching rains.

"I wondered how any person could live many months in Aspinwall," he said, "and wondered still more why any one tried."[4]

As the group traveled west across Panama they were struck by a terrible cholera epidemic. It killed 150 men, women, and children. As the survivors slogged through the damp, humid forest, they had to stop nearly every mile to bury another victim in a shallow, muddy grave. Grant never forgot the horror of that trip.

When he became the eighteenth president of the United States in 1869, Grant ordered surveying expeditions to explore possible routes for a canal. Organized by Commodore Daniel Ammen, chief of the navy's Navigation Bureau, the expeditions visited possible sites in Mexico, Nicaragua, the Panama isthmus, and elsewhere.

Grant appointed an Interoceanic Canal Commission to evaluate their findings. In 1876 the commission recommended the Nicaraguan route, but no further action was taken during Grant's presidency.

The nineteenth president, Rutherford B. Hayes, announced, "The policy of this country is a canal under American control."[5] This aggressive policy defied the Clayton-Bulwer Treaty, but it was not pursued by subsequent administrations. Soon a new player emerged in the quest for the Panama Canal: France.

France wanted to establish a presence in the Western Hemisphere, and a French-built canal would serve that purpose. The French believed that they were the world's premier canal builders, having recently completed the Suez Canal.

From 1859 to 1869, France had built the 100-mile Suez Canal, which joined the Mediterranean Sea to the Gulf of Suez. Many had thought it would be impossible to build the canal, but under the command of de Lesseps, the project had succeeded. This was a source of enormous pride for France. When the country's Committee for Cutting the Interoceanic Canal was founded in the mid-1870s to consider a canal joining the Atlantic and Pacific oceans, de Lesseps was made its president.

In 1876 a friend of de Lesseps's, French navy lieutenant Lucien Napoleon-Bonaparte Wyse (a grandnephew of Napoleon Bonaparte), went to

Panama. When he returned to France, he told the committee that a canal could be built through the isthmus, but it would require using locks, chambers that could be flooded and drained. These would let a ship sail across waterways in the interior of the isthmus, high above sea level.

De Lesseps was not a trained engineer. He didn't want to hear about complicated locks. The Suez was at sea level the entire way. He insisted that the Panama Canal would be, too. He sent Wyse back to Panama with a clear idea of the type of canal he wanted to build.

In 1878 Wyse again returned to France. He brought with him an agreement with the government of Colombia, which owned the land through which the canal would pass. Wyse had also negotiated an agreement with the directors of the Panama railroad for permission to use its right-of-way for the canal.

The committee called for an international convention to discuss the canal. It met on May 15, 1879, in Paris. Many of de Lesseps's friends and

A Panama Railroad train stops at Summit Station in 1855.

Laying tracks through the rain forest was an engineering marvel in itself. Using the railroad's right-of-way would save canal engineers time and trouble.

admirers were delegates. They enthusiastically supported the idea of a sea-level canal because that was the type Le Grand Français recommended. Unfortunately, most of them weren't engineers.[6]

On May 29 the committee voted down a plan for a canal with locks that was proposed by Adolphe Godin de Lépinay, an engineer from France's Department of Public Works. Instead members approved a plan for a sea-level canal.

The seventy-four-year-old de Lesseps brought the convention to its feet when he cried: "Yes! And I accept the command of the enterprise!"[7]

One of de Lesseps's first tasks was to raise money for the company he planned to establish to build the canal. Company shares were priced at 500 francs apiece—an enormous sum when the average industrial worker earned only five francs per day.[8] De Lesseps pointed with pride to Suez: Those shares had also sold for 500 francs. Now they were commanding 2,000 francs apiece.[9] A fund drive was held in the summer of 1879. It raised only 30 million francs. De Lesseps had hoped to raise 400 million francs.

Instead of scaling back his plans, de Lesseps swung into action. On December 30, 1879, he visited Panama for the first time. It was the beginning of Panama's five-month dry season, and the weather was perfect. For six weeks de Lesseps attended a round of parties, official celebrations, concerts, and dances that would have exhausted most seventy-five-year-olds. He thrived on the public adulation.

On February 14, 1880, de Lesseps received a report from his survey team. Nothing he read diminished his confidence. "Panama will be easier to build, easier to finish, and easier to maintain than Suez," he said.[10]

Then he embarked on a six-month, worldwide speaking tour to sell more people on the idea of the canal. Still riding the popularity of his Suez success, de Lesseps found enthusiastic crowds wherever he went. In New York he told an audience exactly how he felt about canals with locks.

"If the committee had decided to build a locked canal, I would have put on my hat and gone home," he said. "Locks are very good for small vessels, but they would not do for large ships."[11]

His efforts paid off. He returned to France in the autumn of 1880 and made a second attempt at fundraising. This time he gained 600 million francs. As with the Suez Canal, it was small French investors—people who idolized de Lesseps—who made the bond issue a success. Eighty thousand people bought one to five shares each. Working-class citizens were gambling everything they had on de Lesseps's success.

Everything seemed to be falling into place. De Lesseps would not even allow the warning words of his engineer son, Charles, to dissuade him:

"What do you hope to gain from Panama?" Charles asked. "At Suez you only succeeded by a miracle; so why not be content with one miracle in your life time rather than hope for another?"[12]

De Lesseps launched his Panama Canal Company at the end of January 1881. Forty French engineers arrived in Panama. Several brought their wives to what had been described as "among the healthiest regions in the world."[13] Housing for workers was built on concrete piers to combat floods and insects. Hospitals described as among the finest in the world were set up. Equipment was ordered, and excavations began at numerous sites. By December 1881, there were 2,000 men at work on the canal.

One simple necessity was overlooked because no one understood its importance: Windows in the workers' houses were not screened. Mosquitoes carrying yellow fever and other deadly diseases were able to fly in and out. Eighty-five workers died in the first year. No one knew then how high the death toll would skyrocket.

Disease was one of the few dreary notes in an otherwise ebullient meeting of the Panama Canal Company on June 29, 1882. The work was going splendidly. De Lesseps poked fun at critics of the project and received a rousing vote of confidence from the shareholders.

He didn't know about another looming problem. His company had hired dozens of subcontractors. There was money flowing on the isthmus, and many people—some honest, some not—wanted their share. The contracts written by the Panama Canal Company were carelessly worded and shot through with costly loopholes.

With these problems still at bay, the company wrote an upbeat summary of the work in December 1882 without knowing how wrong it was: "And so, less than two years after the company's formation, the working force is in position all along the line of the canal . . . [and when] contractors have dug to a certain depth along the whole line of the canal, the rest of the work will be easy."[14]

FYInfo
FOR YOUR INFORMATION

When Napoleon Bonaparte was in Egypt with his forces at the end of the eighteenth century, he considered building a canal to join the Mediterranean and Red seas. The expense of such a project was too great.

Several decades later, Ferdinand de Lesseps learned of Napoleon's dream and adopted it as his own. Without any real idea of how to do it, he promoted building such a waterway. Great Britain disliked the Frenchman's idea because they didn't want their enemy, France, to gain the advantages the canal would provide.

The canal seemed like nothing more than wishful thinking by de Lesseps until 1854, when Sa'id Pasha became the viceroy of Egypt. De Lesseps knew Sa'id quite well from his years as a French diplomat in Egypt. He and Sa'id came to an agreement for building a sea-level canal, and in 1859 the project was launched.

Although not a professional engineer, de Lesseps was a master organizer and promoter, and work progressed steadily. One of the most significant obstacles occurred when Great Britain tried to disrupt the work by stirring up a revolt among the canal's slave laborers. De Lesseps struck back by sending a letter to the British government, asking why it wasn't outraged about the use of involuntary labor to build a British railway through Egypt.

The canal was completed in 1869. On November 17, France's Empress Eugenie officially opened the waterway. The building of the canal was considered as monumental a feat as the construction of the pyramids, and de Lesseps was lionized throughout the world. Great Britain eventually bought all of Sa'id's shares in the canal when they became profitable, and switched from being an opponent of the waterway to being a promoter.

Ironically, the success of Suez led de Lesseps to believe that he could duplicate it in Panama, despite vast differences between the two locations. It was this overconfidence that led to disaster in Panama.

The port city of Colón during the early days of the French attempt to build the canal. Colón was a primitive, disease-filled nightmare.

Years earlier, Ulysses S. Grant had wondered why anyone would ever come to Colón. Nevertheless, it was the closest thing Panama had to a major city on the Atlantic coast, so the French made it the headquarters for their canal-building operation. It was a decision they would come to regret.

A Dream Becomes a Nightmare

In January 1883 the first real sign of trouble occurred in Panama. In that month the French firm Couvreux and Hersent, which was the primary company for the canal job, unexpectedly withdrew. The reason it quit just when excavation was to start is a mystery. It is possible that once the preliminary work was done, members of the firm realized that a sea-level canal would not work.

Jules Dingler, a forty-seven-year-old engineer with experience building roads and bridges but not canals, was chosen as the new overseer of the project. He got the work underway, but things began to go horribly wrong.

One problem was that the Panama Canal Company bought the equipment needed for the work and then rented it to the subcontractors building the canal. The company had to make frequent payments on equipment that wasn't always frequently used. The equipment often piled up on the docks at Colón, the main harbor on the Atlantic. It sat there, useless, because it could not be moved to the work sites fast enough.

Colón itself was a problem. More a collection of wooden buildings than an actual city, Colón had no sewers, wells, or sanitary facilities. It seemed to exist mainly to entice exhausted workers with gambling, prostitution, and drinking.

Another problem was soil excavation. As the digging progressed and cubic yard after cubic yard was dug out of the ground, finding places to dump the soil grew increasingly difficult. When the land on the sides of the canal trench was flat, the soil could be carried there by long chutes. But when the ground was higher than the trench, it became almost impossible to dispose of the dirt. Each subcontractor was responsible for finding its own disposal site, and that usually meant transporting it by railroad and dumping it somewhere in the rain forest. Sometimes the excavated soil was dumped near the trench. That meant another subcontractor had to excavate it all over again.[1]

These unplanned and largely unsupervised excavations led to a series of loose, unstable hills of soil that were prone to landslides. The longer the digging went on, the greater the problem became. The torrential rains increased the danger. No one knew when a sudden rainstorm would cause thousands of cubic feet of earth to come cascading down into the excavated canal channel.

One area in particular, known as the Culebra Cut, was incredibly difficult to excavate. This was an eight-mile area of highlands near the Pacific Ocean. To cut through this section, the French estimated that they would have to move 22 million cubic yards of earth and rock. Here the landslide problem was particularly evident. The initial company contracted for the cut wound up excavating only 810,000 cubic yards because of continued landslides.[2]

Disease was another huge problem. Some estimate that in the isthmus's Chagres Valley, the wettest section of the country, as many as six out of every seven Europeans came down with malaria or yellow fever.[3] In other areas the problem was just as bad. One French engineer said, "Death was constantly gathering its harvest all about me. Within a stone's-throw of my house in Colón, ships were anchored in the harbor without a single person aboard: their whole crew had died. I especially remember twelve English sailors, in full uniform, waiting to see the doctor; within the week every one of them was dead."[4]

Chief overseer Dingler was among those from whom yellow fever exacted a terrible price. Boasting that he was bringing his family to Panama to prove that only those of lesser character died of yellow fever, he watched horrified as the disease killed his son, daughter, son-in-law, and finally his wife. Stunned, he led the horses that his family had loved riding into the mountains and shot them. In the summer of 1885 he returned to France, a hollow shell of his former self. He died soon afterward.

Another problem no one anticipated was the effect of the rain. The dry season in Panama lasted from mid-December through April. Then in May the heavens opened and did not shut again for months. It rained almost every day, turning the ground into mush and the air to soup. The never-ending dampness caused expensive iron and steel machinery to rust in a matter of days. Workers' shoes grew mold overnight.

Any of these problems would have been difficult to solve. Combined, they seemed impossible to overcome.

As news from the isthmus grew more alarming, worried shareholders of the Panama Canal Company in July 1885 suggested that de Lesseps return there and try to right the situation. He timed his visit for February 1886—the dry season—when he gave more stirring speeches, galloped around on a horse encouraging everyone, and visited workers to witness firsthand the problems. Within a couple of months, de Lesseps realized that he would need more money. He issued more bonds, hoping to raise another 600 million francs. News of setbacks on the project dampened investors' enthusiasm. De Lesseps only raised 354 million francs.

Another problem that had nothing to do with conditions in Panama but was endemic of the times in France was corruption. Newspaper reporters wanted money for writing favorable stories, and editors wanted more money to run them. Just one positive line in print resulted in someone holding out their hand for payment. A significant amount of money that should have gone toward the project was diverted to bribes for newspapers, public officials, and others. Eventually more than 2,500 newspapers and magazines were paid off.[5]

Corruption in Panama was rampant. Most machinery ran on coal. A coal ship would dock, unload a portion of its coal, and demand payment for the entire amount. The ship would then sail out to sea, turn around, dock again, and once again charge full price for a partial load. One ship could be paid for several loads of cargo when it had delivered only one.

If de Lesseps had seen the writing on the wall and consented to a canal with locks, he might have saved the situation. Even in early 1887, however, the stubborn de Lesseps refused to admit that the sea-level Suez Canal could not be replicated in Panama. Work floundered on.

Finally in November of 1887, de Lesseps grudgingly agreed to a canal with temporary locks. He signed a contract with famed engineer Alexandre Gustave Eiffel to build them. De Lesseps had come around too late. Switching to a canal with locks would cost another 500 million francs, and it was money that his company didn't have.

The French people had provided over one billion francs to build a sea-level canal. Now de Lesseps was proclaiming that a lock-style canal, which he had spent years deriding, was what was needed in Panama. During most of 1888 the Panama Canal Company scrambled for funds, but investors had become wary of the project. De Lesseps and his son Charles again launched one of their whirlwind speaking tours in the autumn of 1888, urging the sale of the company's bonds. The tour was not a success—the de Lesseps magic had disappeared.

In December 1888 the Panama Canal Company collapsed. The company's failure hit France like a bomb. Small investors who had supported de Lesseps financially were devastated; thousands of people lost everything. It was history's biggest bankruptcy. The word *Panama* became a French synonym for corruption.

Inevitably much of the blame fell upon de Lesseps. The failure of the project transformed him overnight from an energetic dynamo to a frail shadow of his former self. He went weeks without talking, became wheelchair-bound, and spent his last years sitting silently in front of the fireplace or in his garden at home, his mind dwelling on past glories.

The Panama Canal project he had championed was described as "the greatest fraud of modern times"[6] by the prosecutor at his trial. De Lesseps and his son Charles were sentenced to five years in prison and a fine of 3,000 francs. The old man was allowed to remain at his home in his dotage. Charles, who had tried to divert the blame from his father onto himself, served six months before being released for health reasons.

After the collapse of the Panama Canal Company, work proceeded fitfully on the project for a few more months. On May 15, 1889, all work stopped. The giant dredges and other machinery became still. An eerie quiet settled over the formerly bustling isthmus. Nearly 14,000 workers were no longer employed.

On December 7, 1894, Ferdinand de Lesseps died at the age of eighty-nine. The man was dead, but had his dream also perished?

Canals are usually built to connect bodies of water: the Panama Canal connects the Atlantic and Pacific oceans. When a canal connects bodies of water at different levels, a system of locks is used to enable a boat to move through it. A lock is basically a big waterproof box. The box must be large enough to hold an entire ship. Gates on each end of the lock allow the ship to enter and exit.

Let's say a canal has to traverse a hill to get to a lake at the top. A series of three locks is set into the canal along the hill: a low, middle, and high lock. A boat that needs to get to the top of the hill will sail into the low lock, and the gate will close behind it (1). Vents in the gate between the first lock and the middle lock are opened. Water from the middle lock pours through the vents into the low lock, filling it up and lifting the boat (2). (The gate at the other end of the low lock keeps the water in.) When the water level in the low lock matches the level in the middle lock, the gate opens between these two locks (3) and the boat sails into the middle lock (4). The process is repeated until the ship reaches the top lock and can continue its journey. If a boat is going the other way, the process is reversed.

By using vents, valves, or pumps to get water into or out of a lock, a boat can be moved up or down to the level of the next lock or waterway. Sometimes these distances can be great. For example, the Panama Canal's series of locks lift or lower a boat an incredible eighty-five feet. Once you know that, you can see why the original plan to build the Panama Canal without locks was doomed to fail.

Locks are found in canals all over the world, from the smallest to the biggest. There are numerous types of locks, such as staircase locks, paired locks, and drop locks. Locks are some of engineering's most unique and useful inventions.

Panama Canal Miraflores locks. Locks help canals regulate the water level, and ensure that ships will have a smooth journey all the way through the waterway.

Culebra Cut during the 1888 collapse of the Panama Canal. The Culebra Cut was where the most difficult work took place during the digging of the canal.

The Culebra Cut had defied French efforts to tame it. Dirt continually slid down the sides of the mountains, filling in areas that had already been dug out. It took widening the cut, and 400,000 pounds of dynamite per month, for the Americans to solve the problem.

Roosevelt Wants a Canal

While people in the United States liked and admired de Lesseps, the general feeling in America was relief that "foreigners" had not successfully completed the canal.[1] Within a few months of the French failure, the New York–based Nicaraguan Canal Company was hard at work building a canal in Nicaragua. After digging a trench less than a mile long, it too went bankrupt.

The failure of both companies quieted the clamor for a canal. Then in April 1898 the Spanish-American War erupted. The American battleship *Oregon* left San Francisco in March on its way to the Caribbean in anticipation of the conflict. By the time the ship arrived sixty-eight days later, after her long journey around the southern tip of South America, the war was virtually over. It became crystal clear to Americans that a quicker route from west to east was needed.

The United States formed the Walker Commission in 1899 to study possible canal routes. In 1901 the commission came out in favor of a Nicaraguan canal. This was terrible news to stockholders of the New Panama Canal Company, which had purchased the assets of the failed Panama Canal Company. If it could sell its right-of-way, equipment, and other holdings to the United States for a Panama-based canal, it stood to make a lot of money. If not, it would be stuck with a huge earthen ditch and rusting construction equipment.

Two men—William Nelson Cromwell, a New York lawyer representing the company, and Philippe Bunau-Varilla, a stockholder—swung into action. They waged an intense lobbying campaign in the U.S. Congress on behalf of the Panama site. Their lobbying worked. In June 1902, the U.S. Senate passed the Spooner Act authorizing the government to build a canal in Panama.

Another key piece of the puzzle had fallen into place six months earlier, when the U.S. Senate approved the Hay-Pauncefote Treaty in December 1901.

This treaty superseded the Clayton-Bulwer Treaty of 1850. It freed the United States to construct and operate a Central American canal without Great Britain as long as the waterway was accessible to all nations.

The Spooner Act gave the U.S. government permission to acquire the land from Colombia—known as the Canal Zone—on which to build the canal. The U.S. Secretary of State and Colombian officials negotiated a treaty that would let the United States buy the land for $10 million and give Colombia annual tolls of $250,000. In March 1903 the U.S. Senate ratified the treaty, but the Colombian government delayed and finally rejected the treaty on August 12, 1903. It wanted more than $10 million.

The treaty's defeat angered both U.S. President Theodore Roosevelt and the people of Panama. More than once, the region of Panama had tried to separate from Colombia. In October 1903 Bunau-Varilla spoke to American officials—including President Roosevelt—and told them that another revolution in Panama was likely. Bunau-Varilla came away convinced that the United States would support the rebels, and he communicated that feeling to them. On October 30, 1903, the naval cruiser *Nashville* was sent down to Colón.

Three days later, the *Nashville* appeared in Colón's harbor. Panama's rebels were emboldened by this apparent show of U.S. support. Later in the day, when the Colombian gunboat *Cartagena* arrived in the harbor, the rebels were not afraid. The next day, November 3, Panama declared its independence. Within forty-eight hours the U.S. recognized the new government of Panama.

For a few tense days it seemed as if warfare might break out between the United States and Colombia, but Colombia knew it was facing a much more powerful foe. It withdrew, paving the way for the Republic of Panama to be declared on November 6, 1903. Two weeks later a new canal treaty was negotiated. The United States made out far better than it had when it was negotiating with Colombia. By the end of February 1904 the treaty had been ratified by both the Panamanian and U.S. governments.

The treaty had been negotiated for Panama by Bunau-Varilla. It is a mystery how Bunau-Varilla, a private citizen who owned stock in the New Panama Canal Company, was able to persuade Panama to let him negotiate on its behalf. Bunau-Varilla, who had never written a treaty before, inserted many clauses to make it favorable to the United States. Secretary of State John Hay didn't hesitate to sign the treaty.

The United States came under criticism for supposedly encouraging and supporting the revolution. *The New York Evening Post* blasted the president and Hay for throwing aside the principals of the nation. When Roosevelt protested that the people of the isthmus "rose as one man"[2] to declare independence, a U.S. Senator cracked, "Yes, and the one man was Roosevelt."[3]

Roosevelt defended his actions vigorously, saying that he did nothing improper. Later, however, in a speech at the University of California in 1911, Roosevelt almost seemed to agree with his critics: "Accordingly, I took the Isthmus, started the canal and then left Congress not to debate the canal, but to debate me."[4]

On April 16, 1904, the United States formally assumed the assets of the New Panama Canal Company for $40 million.

In the early summer of 1904, the first U.S. construction crews arrived in Panama. Roosevelt had named a seven-member Isthmian Canal Commission to head the project. Success seemed guaranteed, but it was not to be. The commissioners argued furiously among themselves and could not agree on anything. For instance, in August 1904, chief engineer John Wallace ordered sewage pipes. The commission argued about the request for months before finally ordering the pipes in December. By the time the pipes were delivered in April 1905, the trenches for the pipes had caved in. In another instance, the commission bungled an order for 15,000 doors and 15,000 door hinges so badly that what arrived were 12,000 doors and 248,000 hinges.

Housing, sanitation, and food for the workers were not any better. One unhappy worker wrote: "Everyone is afflicted with running sores. We are compelled to sleep in an old shed, six to a room. Rain water is drunk rather than the river water, because it is purer. The meals would sicken a dog. . . ."[5]

Angered by the lack of progress, Roosevelt fired the commission and appointed a new one. He made the chief engineer a member, but that didn't make Wallace happy. He had never liked Panama; rumor had it that he was so terrified of yellow fever he had brought along two metal coffins—one for him and one for his wife.

In July 1905 Wallace resigned, after he was turned down for a raise that would have brought his salary to $60,000.

The future of the canal teetered in the balance. If the wrong choice was made for a replacement chief engineer, the project might fail. John Frank

Stevens was chosen. Stevens, a native of Maine, was fifty-two years old and seemed as tough as leather. He had once eluded hostile Apaches for a hundred miles on foot, nearly freezing to death in the Rocky Mountains. The hazards of Panama did not frighten him.

Roosevelt met with Stevens and told him bluntly that the Panama Canal project was in a "devil of a mess."[6] Nearly $130 million had been spent with no results. The ghost of de Lesseps hung heavy over the project. The president admitted that he had no idea what Stevens should do, but said he was reminded of the man who hired a butler and said: "I don't know in the least what you are to do, but . . . you get busy and buttle like hell!"[7]

Stevens arrived in Panama in late July 1905. He lived in a small house instead of the chief engineer's mansion that was being built. He stopped all construction and traipsed through the mud, puffing on big cigars and inspecting every facet of the operation. What he did next surprised some people. Instead

John Frank Stevens was the man who got the Panama Canal project on track.

When Stevens was given the job of Chief Engineer of the Panama Canal, he straightened things out not by digging the canal, but by concentrating on worker conditions.

of restarting the digging, he concentrated on other areas: housing, transportation, equipment, improved sanitation, and disease prevention.

Dr. William Gorgas knew that things were going to improve once Stevens arrived. The chief sanitary officer had been pleading to have mosquito breeding grounds eliminated in order to control disease. His pleas had fallen on deaf ears before Stevens took over, but the new chief engineer listened carefully. Then he gave Dr. Gorgas full authority to eradicate the pests.

Gorgas immediately dispatched thousands of men to destroy the insect and its swampy breeding grounds. In 1905 there were 206 reported cases of yellow fever; in 1906 there was one.[8] Malaria affected an incredible 82 percent of the workforce in 1906. It dropped to 22 percent in 1909 and continued to diminish after that.[9]

Churches, ball fields, and clubhouses were built for the workers. Stevens brought in refrigeration equipment so that food wouldn't spoil in the heat. A

Like the prehistoric bones of some giant animals, the machines were left to the elements, rotting and deteriorating in the rain forest. Their recovery would play a key role when digging resumed.

When the French abandoned the Panama Canal project, they left behind much of their machinery.

new sewage disposal facility was built. More homes were built. Morale among the workers soared.

Perhaps Stevens's biggest challenge was to convince Roosevelt and the U.S. Congress that a canal with locks should be built instead of a sea-level canal. Despite de Lesseps's failure, a sea-level canal was still considered ideal. The vision of a shining ribbon of water running from ocean to ocean and filled with ships was irresistible to many. Stevens himself had once thought a sea-level canal was preferable. After he had been to Panama, stomped over the mushy ground, and seen the untamed Chagres River, he thought differently. He realized that a sea-level canal was "an impracticable futility."[10]

Early in 1906 Stevens told the canal commission and Roosevelt of the feasibility of a lock canal. He pointed out that a lock canal would cost less in maintenance and operation, would need less digging, and could be completed in nine years. A sea-level canal might take eighteen years or longer, if it could be built at all.

In the spring of 1906 Stevens testified before Congress as to why a lock canal was the right choice. The final vote, taken by the Senate on June 21, was thirty-six to thirty-one in favor of a lock canal. By just a few votes, the United States had averted a probable disaster in Panama. Later it was remarked that there was not enough money in the world to build a sea-level canal there.

Finally, after years of false starts, millions of dollars spent, and thousands of lives lost, the right type of canal was to be built on the isthmus.

Ironically, John Stevens would not be the man to build it.

Gatun Locks in the Panama Canal. The decision to build a canal with locks saved the canal project.

Why did the United States build a canal in Panama after the French failure there, and after favoring a route through Nicaragua? There are numerous reasons, but none is more important than the efforts of a Frenchman named Philippe Bunau-Varilla.

Bunau-Varilla was born in Paris on July 26, 1859. After an early career in public works, he took a job with Ferdinand de Lesseps's Panama Canal Company in 1884 as an engineer and worked on the isthmus. The bankruptcy and national humiliation at France's failure to build the canal hit Bunau-Varilla hard. It became his obsession to vindicate de Lesseps's vision by having the canal built. He helped form the New Panama Canal Company, which bought the assets of the failed French company. With help from the New Panama Canal Company's attorney, William Nelson Cromwell, Bunau-Varilla lobbied the American government to place the canal in Panama instead of Nicaragua.

Bunau-Varilla knew how to play the political game. When the U.S. Senate was preparing to vote on where to place the canal, he blanketed the Senate with postage stamps showing a Nicaraguan volcano erupting. For one thing, the volcano was dormant. For another, it wasn't anywhere near the site of the proposed canal, but the stamp had the desired effect. It led decision makers to believe that the Nicaraguan site was dangerous.

When the treaty between Colombia and the U.S. failed, Bunau-Varilla actively promoted Panama's revolution, even to the point of financing it himself. Without official sanction, he drafted a declaration of independence for Panama, got his wife to sew a new flag for the country, and helped prod the U.S. into supporting the rebels. With the revolution over, he then single-handedly negotiated a new treaty for the canal with the United States.

Bunau-Varilla subsequently fought for France in World War I, and lost a leg in battle. He died in Paris on May 18, 1940, just before his beloved France was occupied by Germany in World War II.

Construction of the Panama Canal at Culebra Cut in 1907. Building the Panama Canal was a massive effort involving man and machines versus the elements.

Under the direction of Goethals, excavated dirt was hauled far from the dig by cars on tracks, greatly reducing the cave-ins that plagued workers in the 1880s.

CHAPTER 5

Finally, A Canal

In November 1906 President Roosevelt went to Panama to see how the work was progressing. It was the first time a sitting president had ever left the country, and the trip garnered tremendous publicity. With a new streamlined command structure in place and Stevens in charge, the canal seemed to be on track. For three days Roosevelt waded through mud, walked through puddles, clambered over railroad ties, and talked to workers. "You are doing the biggest thing of the kind that has ever been done," he said to the men, "and I wanted to see how you are doing it."[1]

Back home early in 1907, Roosevelt was happy and confident about the canal. He was thunderstruck on February 12, 1907, when he received a letter from Stevens complaining of political second-guessing, hardship for him and his family, and the strain of the project. Although Stevens did not specifically offer his resignation, Roosevelt realized the chief engineer could not continue in the post in his state of mind. He sent Stevens a cable in which he accepted his resignation. To this day, theories abound as to why Stevens quit. The simplest is that he was exhausted after working so hard to get the canal going. Once everything was in place, he could afford to turn the project over to someone else.

That someone was George Washington Goethals, a forty-eight-year-old member of the Army Corps of Engineers. Like Stevens, Goethals was a no-nonsense sort of man. When asked how he amused himself, the answer came back that he did not amuse himself.[2] It was clear that he could be counted on to continue along the path Stevens had blazed. Unlike Stevens, Goethals was a military man to whom the idea of quitting a task before it was complete was abhorrent.

Roosevelt climbed aboard a steam shovel and interviewed its driver at the Culebra Cut in 1906.

The president inspected the site, learned how the drills and work trains operated, and was given a demonstration of dynamite. He also visited workers in their quarters.

By April 1907, Goethals was in charge. Most of the preliminary work had been done: Disease had been brought under control, the transportation system for moving workers and excavated material had greatly improved, and the idea of a lock canal rather than a sea-level canal had been accepted. Now the biggest problem remaining was digging the dirt—about 220 million cubic yards of it.[3]

Goethals got busy. At times more dirt was moved in a single day than had been done previously in a month. At its peak, the excavations under Goethals were the same as if the Suez Canal were being dug every three years. At the Culebra Cut, dozens of steam shovels worked daily. Railroad cars ran virtually nonstop to take the dirt away.

Initially Goethals was resented by the workers. He had neither the easygoing personality of Stevens, nor his bonds with the men. His fairness, honesty, and hard work ethic soon won them over. He established a newspaper for the workers. He instituted an excavation contest for the steam shovels and dredges that got the men working even harder. He had an open-door policy of hearing worker grievances every Sunday morning.

Goethals divided the work into three sections: the Atlantic division, the central division, and the Pacific division. By far the most intense work took place in the central division at the Culebra Cut. There, dirt had repeatedly slid down the mountainsides into the newly excavated ditch. The problem was solved by enlarging the cut to a width of 1,800 feet—nearly three times wider than originally envisioned. Only by making it that much bigger were the Americans able to move enough dirt to stop landslides. Ultimately 96 million cubic yards of dirt were removed from the cut.[4]

The Culebra Cut was the spectacle of the project. Thousands of people came to watch from several hundred feet above as an army of men and machines swarmed over the cut. The noise level was ear-shattering and constant. Three hundred rock drills, sixty steam shovels, dozens of railroad cars running back and forth, and dynamite blasting away rock produced a thunderous volume of sound. More than 61 million pounds of dynamite were used on the canal (a greater amount of explosives than had been used in all of America's wars up to that point). The Culebra Cut alone took up to 400,000 pounds of dynamite per month.[5]

With that many explosives being used, accidents resulted. The worst occurred on December 12, 1908, when twenty-two tons of dynamite exploded unexpectedly. Twenty-three men were killed, and another forty hurt.

The Chagres River was tamed by building the giant Gatun Dam. (The idea to dam the river had first been suggested by Frenchman Godin de Lépinay in 1879, but his notion had been dismissed.) Gatun Dam was 1.5 miles long and half a mile thick at the base. The dam created the 85-foot-deep Gatun Lake, which at 160 square miles was the world's largest artificial lake at the time. The dam also generated hydroelectric power that powered the canal's lights and locks.

The other piece of the canal puzzle was building the locks. Each of the twelve locks was 110 feet wide and 1,100 feet long. Their side walls were as tall as a six-story building. The locks were designed to work by gravity; water entered the lock from above and drained out below.

After so many false starts, the canal now raced toward completion. In June 1913 Gatun Dam was finished. The locks were tested in September 1913

More than 61 million pounds of dynamite were used during the construction of the Panama Canal.

Since roads in Panama were virtually non-existent, railroad cars were used to haul building supplies in and haul dirt out.

The 85-foot-deep Gatun Lake was made by damming the Chagres River.

In August 1914, the *Ancon* took the first official trip through the recently completed Panama Canal.

and worked perfectly. A few days later a violent earthquake thought to rival the intensity of the San Francisco earthquake of 1906 struck Panama. The canal suffered no damage.

Plans for celebrations to mark the opening of the canal were discussed. Before they could take place, the *Cristobal*, a small cement boat owned by the Panama Railroad Company, made an unceremonious first voyage through the canal on August 3, 1914.

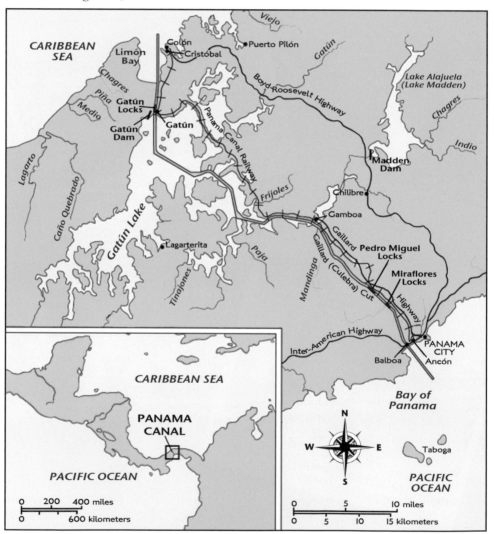

The 50-mile route of the Panama Canal closely follows the route of the Panama Railroad.

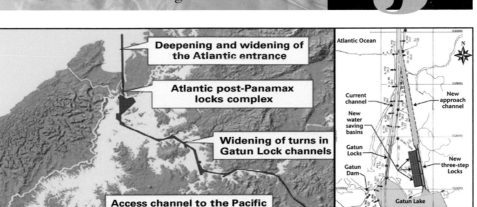

Deepening and widening of
the Atlantic entrance

Atlantic post-Panamax
locks complex

Widening of turns in
Gatun Lock channels

Access channel to the Pacific
post-Panamax locks

Pacific post-Panamax
locks complex

Deepening and widening of
the Pacific entrance

Atlantic Ocean

Current channel
New approach channel
New water saving basins
Gatun Locks
Gatun Dam
New three-step Locks
Gatun Lake

By the twenty-first century, many ships were too large to use the Panama Canal. (Panamax ships are those that barely fit in the canal; post-Panamax ships are larger.) Expansion plans included deepening and widening the entrances and turns in the channels, and using new three-step locks. Water for raising and lowering the ships would be conserved in basins next to the new locks.

The official grand opening trip was performed by a ship called the *Ancon* on August 15, 1914. It took nine hours. On board were several hundred dignitaries. It should have been a historic moment celebrated across the globe, but greater international events were taking place. World War I had begun in Europe, and the attention of the world was diverted. A feat that had been dreamed about for centuries was overshadowed when it was finally accomplished.

In 1921 the United States paid Colombia $25 million for the loss of Panama in what was called a "friendly expression of regret." The movement to pay Colombia, begun during the presidential administration of Woodrow Wilson, infuriated Theodore Roosevelt.

In December 1999 the United States turned over control of the canal to Panama. More and more ships were too large to use the original canal, and in 2008, expansion plans were under way. The Panama Canal is still considered a wonder of the world, and a shining example of what humanity can accomplish for the betterment of all.

Commemoration exercises at Gatun Lock in 1914

Total cost (combined French and American): $639 million

Total fatalities (combined French and American): about 25,000, or 500 lives for every mile of canal

Toll from 1914 to 1973: 90 cents per cargo ton

Toll from 1973 to 1994: $1.08 per cargo ton

Since October 1, 1994, tolls have been based on the Panama Canal Universal Measurement System, which accounts for ship capacity and cargo volume.

Largest toll collected as of 1975: $42,077.88 (*Queen Elizabeth II*); by 2008, oil tankers were routinely paying up to $180,000 in tolls

Smallest toll collected: 36 cents (Richard Halliburton in 1928—he swam the length of the canal)

Length of canal: 50 miles

Time to cross the canal: nine hours

Cost for yearly operation of canal: $450 million

Cost for annual maintenance: $100 million

Number of ships that use the canal annually: 12,000

The Panama Canal in 2008

Chapter Notes

Chapter 1. Never to Smile Again

1. Ian Cameron, *The Building of the Panama Canal* (New York: William Morrow & Company, 1972), p. 94.

2. David McCullough, *The Path Between the Seas* (New York: Simon and Schuster, 1977), p. 200.

3. Ibid., p. 200.

4. Cameron, p. 96.

Chapter 2. The French Attempt a Canal

1. Ian Cameron, *The Building of the Panama Canal* (New York: William Morrow & Company, 1972), p. 24.

2. Ibid., p. 26.

3. Maron J. Simon, *The Panama Affair* (New York: Charles Scribner's Sons, 1971), p. 43.

4. Brooks D. Simpson, *Ulysses S. Grant: Triumph Over Adversity* (New York: Houghton Mifflin Company, 2000), p. 65.

5. Norman J. Padelford, *The Panama Canal in Peace and War* (New York: The Macmillan Company, 1942), p. 12.

6. Cameron, p. 31.

7. Simon, p. 20.

8. Ibid., p. 2.

9. Ibid., p. 2.

10. Cameron, p. 36.

11. Simon, p. 32.

12. Cameron, p. 37.

13. Ibid., p. 40.

14. Ibid., p. 50.

Chapter 3. A Dream Becomes a Nightmare

1. "The Panama Canal: The First Attempt," *History Magazine*, April/May 2007, p. 33.

2. Ian Cameron, *The Building of the Panama Canal* (New York: William Morrow & Company, 1972), p. 73.

3. Ibid., p. 62.

4. Ibid., p. 75.

5. "The Panama Canal: The First Attempt," p. 35.

6. Cameron, p. 101.

Chapter 4. Roosevelt Wants a Canal

1. Ian Cameron, *The Building of the Panama Canal* (New York: William Morrow & Company, 1972), p. 106.

2. David McCullough, *The Path Between the Seas* (New York: Simon and Schuster, 1977), p. 382.

3. Ibid., p. 382.

4. Ibid., p. 384.

5. Cameron, p. 122.

6. McCullough, p. 462.

7. Ibid., p. 462.

8. Cameron, p. 134.

9. Ibid., p. 141.

10. McCullough, p. 485.

Chapter 5. Finally, A Canal

1. David McCullough, *The Path Between the Seas* (New York: Simon and Schuster, 1977), p. 495.

2. Ibid., p. 509.

3. Ian Cameron, *The Building of the Panama Canal* (New York: William Morrow & Company, 1972), p. 171.

4. McCullough, p. 547.

5. Ibid., p. 545.

Chronology

1513 Balboa becomes the first European to see the Pacific Ocean from its eastern shore.

1848 James Marshall discovers gold in California.

1849 The California gold rush begins.

1850 The Clayton-Bulwer Treaty is signed.

1852 Ulysses S. Grant leads an ill-fated trek across the Isthmus of Panama.

1855 The Panama railroad is completed.

1876 The Interoceanic Canal Commission recommends digging a canal through Nicaragua.

1879 De Lesseps calls for a convention to discuss building a canal in Panama.

1880 U.S. President Rutherford B. Hayes declares that the canal should be under American control.

1881 French workers begin digging the Panama Canal.

1888 De Lesseps's Panama Canal Company goes bankrupt in December, ending French efforts to build the canal.

1898 The Spanish-American War makes the value of a canal through Central America clear.

1901 The Hay-Pauncefote Treaty enables America to build a canal in Central America.

1902 A canal route through Panama is approved by the U.S. Senate.

1903 *January*   The U.S. and Colombia negotiate a treaty to allow the U.S. to build a canal in Panama.

        November Panama declares independence from Colombia.

        November The U.S. recognizes the new nation of Panama.

        November The Hay-Bunau-Varilla Treaty gives the U.S. the right to build the Panama Canal.

1904 The U.S. Senate approves a treaty with Panama. America buys the holdings of the New Panama Canal Company.

1905 President Theodore Roosevelt appoints John Stevens as chief engineer in charge of building the Panama Canal.

1906 The U.S. Senate approves a lock-style canal instead of a sea-level one.

1907 George Goethals replaces Stevens as chief engineer.

1913 Work is completed on the Culebra Cut, Gatun Dam, and the locks.

1914 The Panama Canal opens.

1999 U.S. gives control of the canal to Panama.

2007 Work begins on expanding the canal to allow larger ships to pass.

2008 Canal expansion continues to boost Panama's economy.

Timeline in History

1850	The twelfth U.S. president, Zachary Taylor, dies.
1852	*Uncle Tom's Cabin* by Harriet Beecher Stowe is published.
1857	The U.S. Supreme Court issues the Dred Scott decision.
1860	Abraham Lincoln is elected the sixteenth U.S. president.
1861	The Civil War begins.
1863	The Battle of Gettysburg is fought.
1865	The Civil War ends; Abraham Lincoln is assassinated.
1867	The U.S. buys Alaska from Russia.
1869	Ulysses S. Grant becomes the eighteenth U.S. president. The Suez Canal opens.
1871	The Great Chicago Fire destroys four square miles of the city and kills hundreds.
1876	The Battle of Little Bighorn is fought.
1886	The Statue of Liberty is dedicated.
1898	The Spanish-American War is fought.
1898	Hawaii is annexed by the U.S.
1901	Theodore Roosevelt replaces assassinated William McKinley as president.
1903	The Wright brothers make their first flight from Kitty Hawk, South Carolina.
1906	The San Francisco earthquake kills hundreds and devastates the city.
1909	Cherry trees are planted along the banks of the Potomac River.
1914	World War I begins in Europe.
1915	Long-distance telephone service begins.
1917	The U.S. enters World War I.
1918	A worldwide influenza epidemic begins, killing millions and lasting two years.
1918	World War I ends.
1923	The Teapot Dome scandal begins to brew as public land with oil reserves is secretly leased to private companies.
1927	Charles Lindbergh makes the first solo flight across the Atlantic Ocean.
1929	The stock market crashes and heralds the beginning of the Great Depression.
1932	Franklin D. Roosevelt becomes the thirty-second U.S. president.
1939	World War II begins in Europe.
1941	Japan attacks Pearl Harbor and sends the United States into World War II.
1945	World War II ends.
1948	The Marshall Plan is passed to begin rebuilding Europe.

Further Reading

For Young Adults

Anderson, Dale. *Building the Panama Canal.* Milwaukee, Wisconsin: World Almanac Library, 2005.

Bodden, Valerie. *Suez Canal.* Mankato, Minnesota: Creative Education, 2007.

Donnelly, Matt. *Theodore Roosevelt: Larger than Life.* North Haven, Connecticut: Linnet Books, 2003.

Ingram, Scott. *The Panama Canal.* Farmington Hills, Michigan: Blackbirch Press, 2003.

Mann, Elizabeth. *The Panama Canal: The Story of How a Jungle Was Conquered and the World Made Smaller.* New York: Mikaya Press, 2006.

Zimmermann, Warren. *First Great Triumph: How Five Americans Made Their Country a World Power.* New York: Farrar, Straus and Giroux, 2002.

Works Consulted

Balf, Todd. *The Darkest Jungle.* New York: Crown Publishers, 2003.

Cameron, Ian. *The Building of the Panama Canal.* New York: William Morrow & Company, 1972.

McCullough, David. *The Path Between the Seas.* New York: Simon and Schuster, 1977.

Morris, Edmund. *Theodore Rex.* New York: Random House, 2001.

Padelford, Norman J. *The Panama Canal in Peace and War.* New York: The Macmillan Company, 1942.

"The Panama Canal: The First Attempt." *History Magazine,* April/May 2007.

"Panama Rises," *Smithsonian,* March 2004.

Perret, Geoffrey. *Ulysses S. Grant: Soldier & Statesman.* New York: Random House, 1997.

"The President Climbs a Canal Steam Shovel." *New York Times,* November 17, 1906.

Reagan, Brad. "The Panama Canal's Ultimate Upgrade." *Popular Mechanics,* February 2007. Online at: http://www.popularmechanics.com/technology/transportation/4212183.html?page=1

Simon, Maron J. *The Panama Affair.* New York: Charles Scribner's Sons, 1971.

Simpson, Brooks D. *Ulysses S. Grant: Triumph Over Adversity.* New York: Houghton Mifflin Company, 2000.

On the Internet

The Land Divided, the World United—Panama Canal Authority
http://www.pancanal.com

Panama Canal History Museum
http://www.canalmuseum.com

Popular Mechanics: Panama Canal Expansion
http://www.popularmechanics.com/panama

Theodore Roosevelt Association
http://www.theodoreroosevelt.org

Glossary

abhorrent (ab-HOR-ent)—Deserving strong dislike.

basked (BASKT)—Enjoyed a pleasant atmosphere.

buttle (BUH-tul)—To work or serve as a butler.

cholera (KAH-luh-ruh)—A disease marked by diarrhea, vomiting, and cramps.

dissuade (dis-WAYD)—To persuade not to do something.

dotage (DOH-tij)—Feebleness of mind, especially resulting from old age.

dynamo (DY-nuh-moh)—An energetic person.

ebullient (eh-BUL-lyent)—High-spirited.

emboldened (em-BOWL-dend)—Filled with courage.

endemic (en-DEM-ik)—Belonging to a place.

equator (ee-KWAY-tor)—An imaginary line around the earth equal in distance from the North and South poles.

eradicate (eh-RAA-dih-kayt)—To completely destroy.

infuriated (in-FYOOR-ee-ay-ted)—Made angry.

isthmus (ISS-muss)—A narrow strip of land bordered by water and connecting two larger bodies of land.

malaria (muh-LAYR-ee-uh)—A mosquito-borne disease with symptoms of chills, fever, and sweating.

parasols (PAYR-uh-solz)—Umbrellas used to block the sun.

sanction (SANK-shun)—Official permission.

strenuous (STREN-yoo-us)—Very active.

trek (TREK)—To journey slowly or with difficulty.

vigorous (VIH-guh-rus)—Strong and active.

vindicate (VIN-dih-kayt)—To clear from blame.

Index